R0061389524

12/2011

The Essential JIM BRICKMAN

Arranged by Dan Coates

Christmas

Contents

DAN COATES® is a registered trademark of Alfred Music Publishing Co., Inc.
© MMIX by Alfred Music Publishing Co., Inc.
All rights reserved. Printed in USA.

ISBN-10: 0-7390-6271-9
ISBN-13: 978-0-7390-6271-5

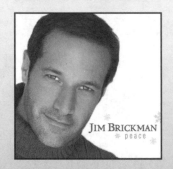
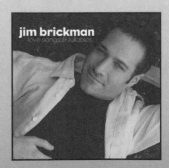

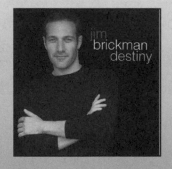

ANGELS

Written by Jim Brickman
Arranged by Dan Coates

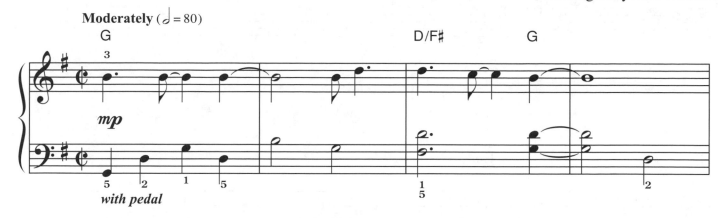

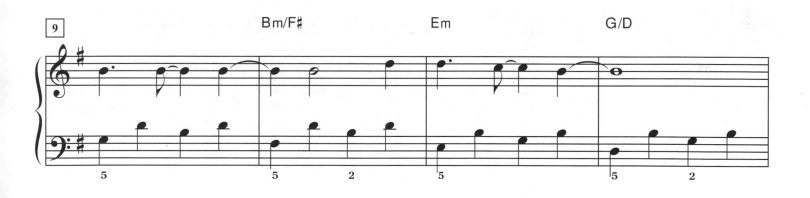

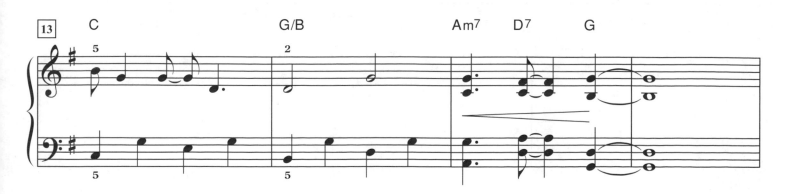

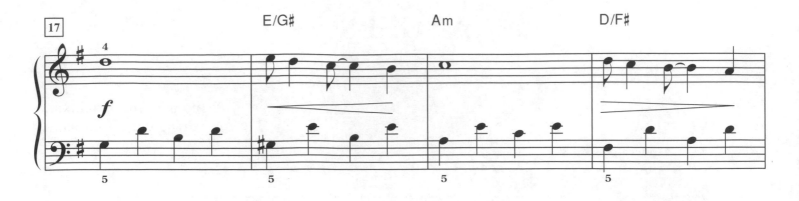

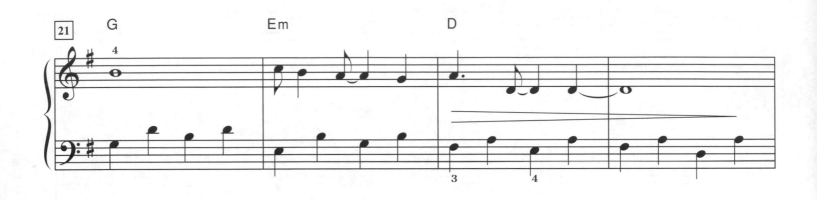

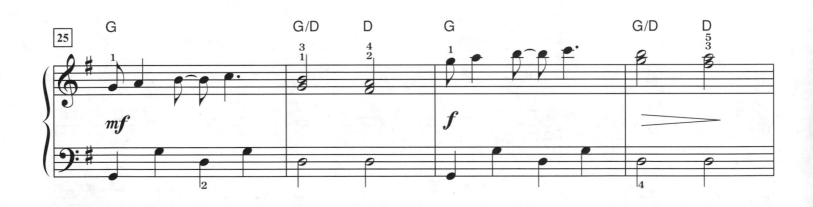

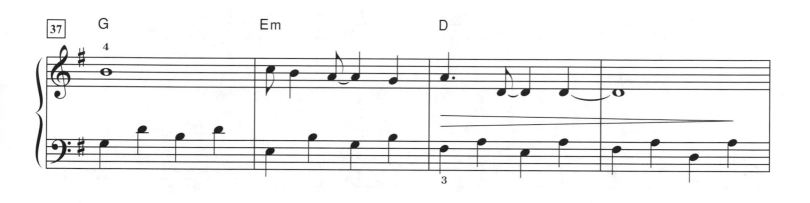

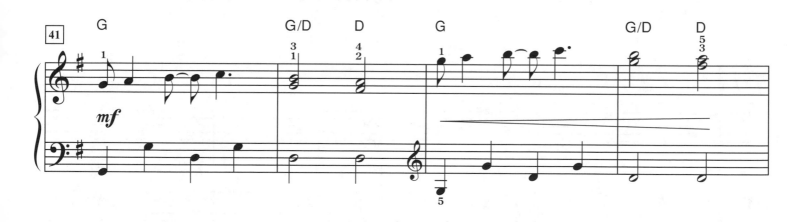

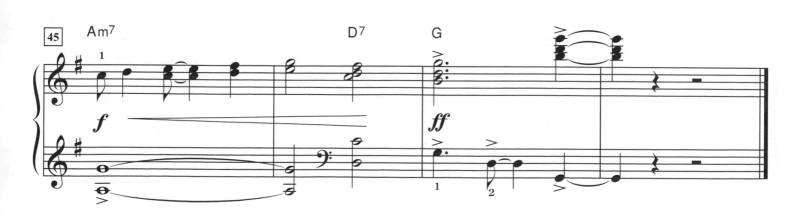

EARLY SNOWFALL

Written by Jim Brickman
Arranged by Dan Coates

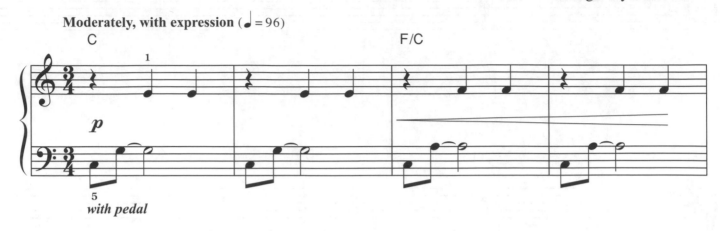

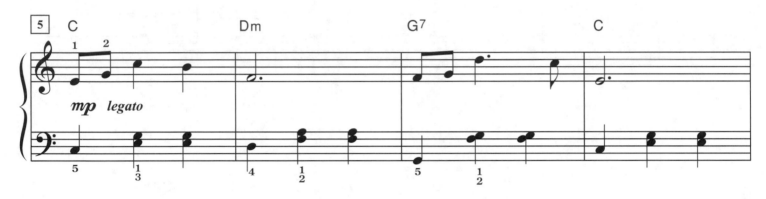

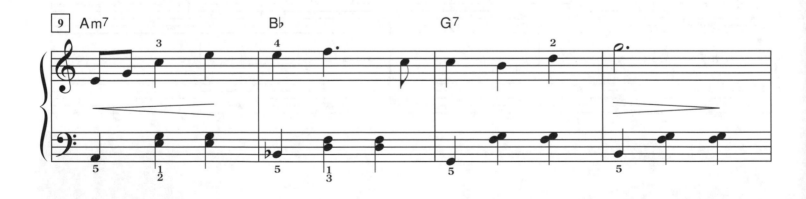

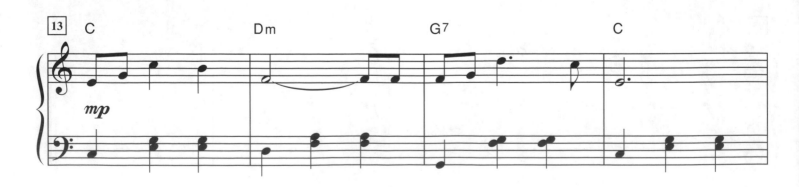

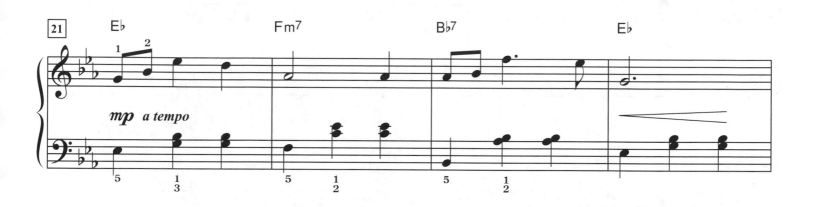

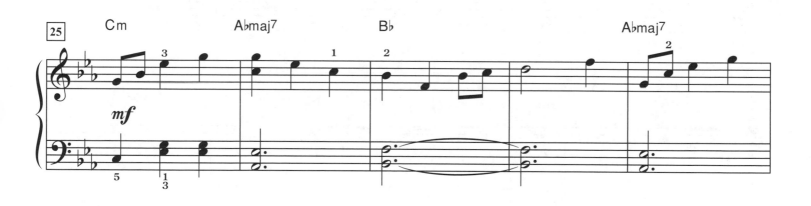

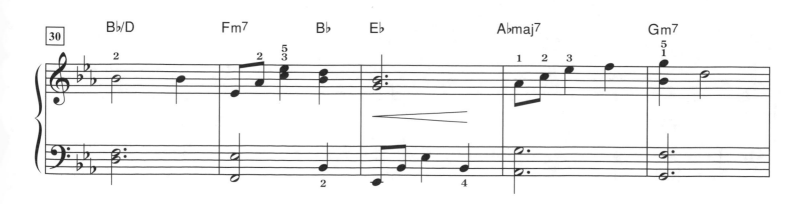

9

EVEN SANTA FELL IN LOVE

Words and Music by
Jim Brickman and Billy Mann
Arranged by Dan Coates

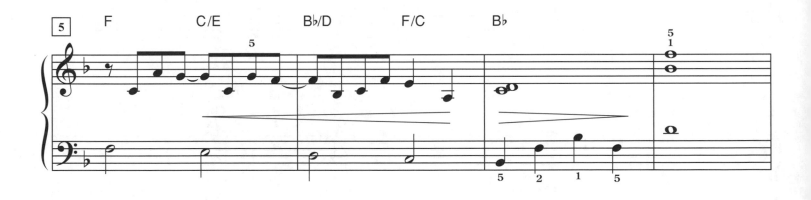

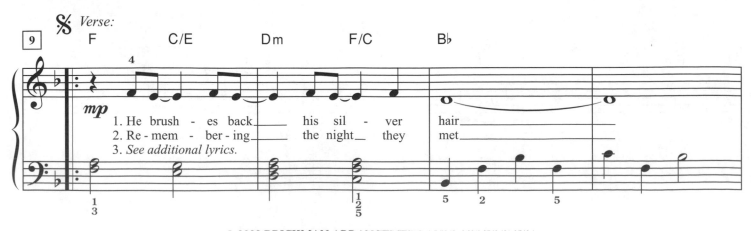

1. He brush - es back___ his sil - ver hair___
2. Re - mem - ber - ing___ the night___ they met___
3. *See additional lyrics.*

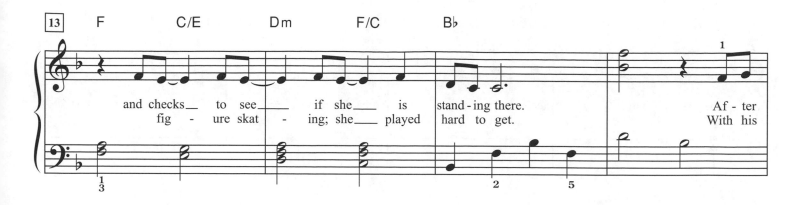

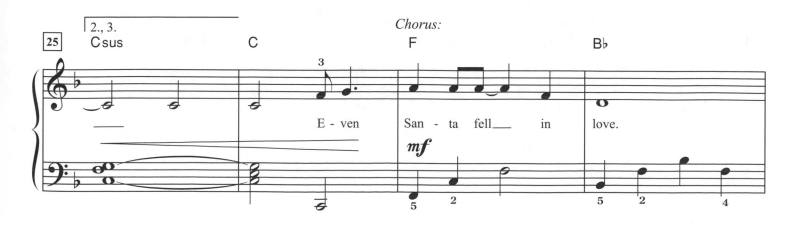

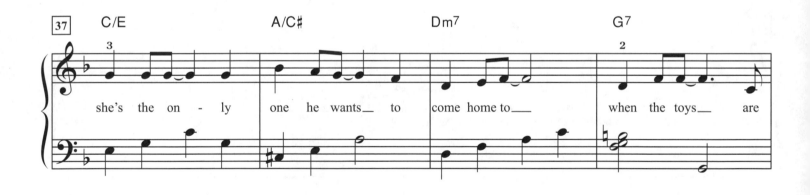

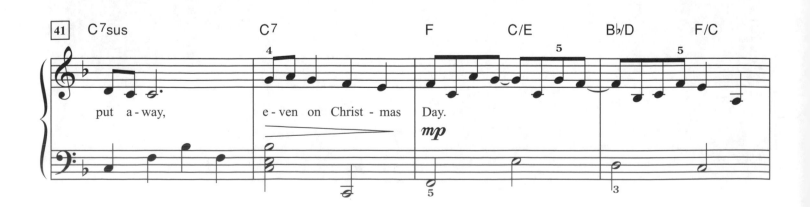

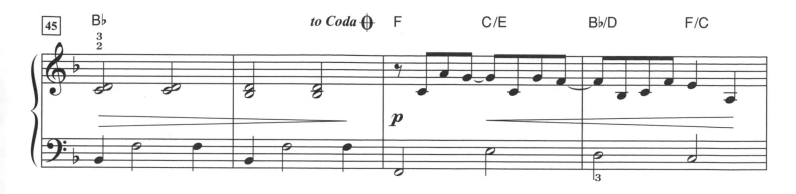

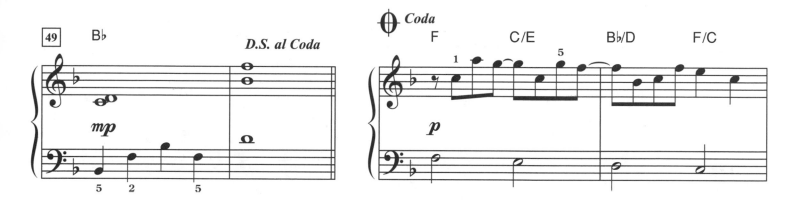

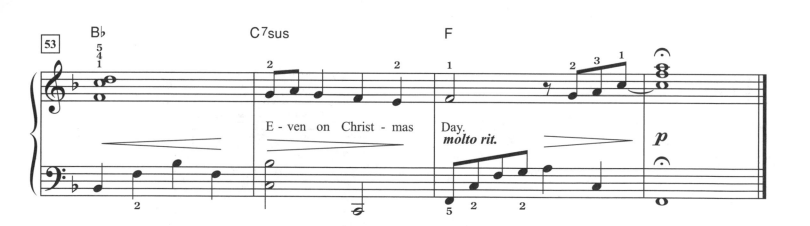

Verse 3:
She sees his eyes are all aglow,
Anticipating children laughing in the snow.
And with just his Christmas touch,
Under mistletoe, before the rush,
Mrs. Kringle feels the tingle in her heart.
(To Chorus:)

THE GIFT

Words and Music by
Jim Brickman and Tom Douglas
Arranged by Dan Coates

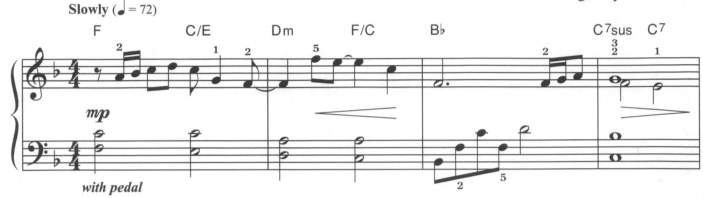

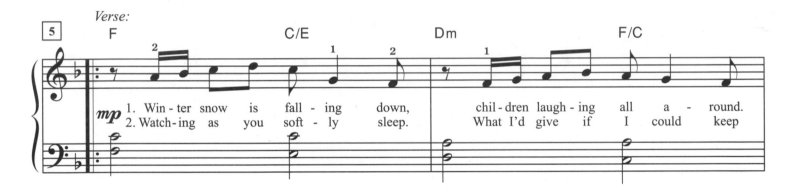

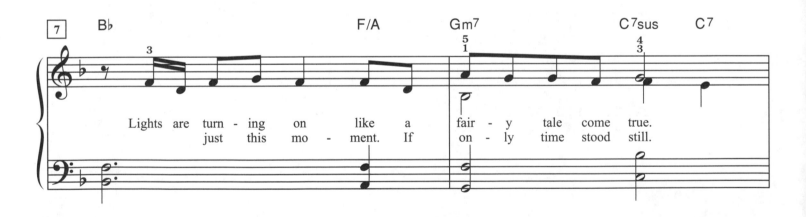

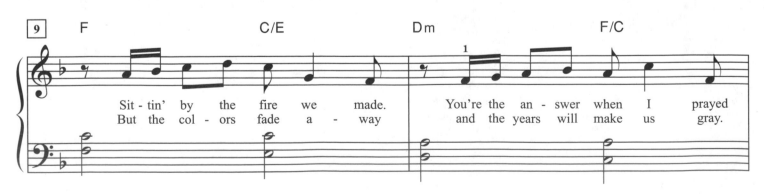

GREENSLEEVES/CAROL OF THE BELLS

(Medley)

Traditional
Arranged by Jim Brickman
Arranged by Dan Coates

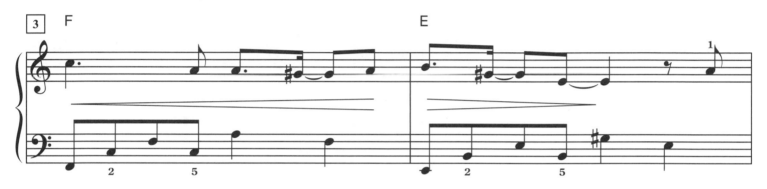

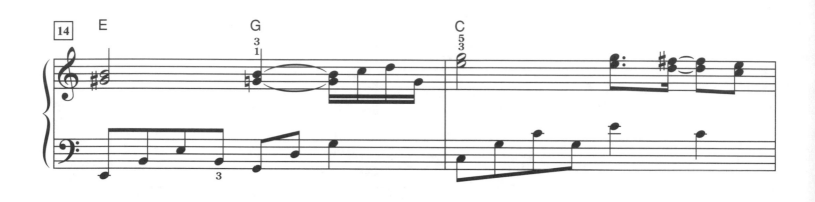

HARK! THE HERALD ANGELS SING

Traditional
Arranged by Jim Brickman
Arranged by Dan Coates

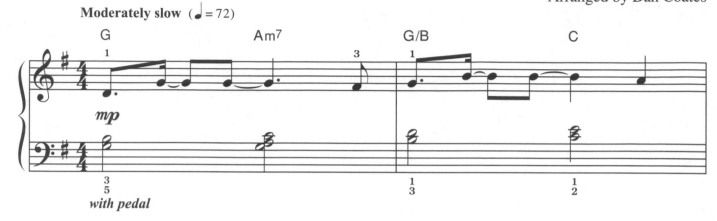

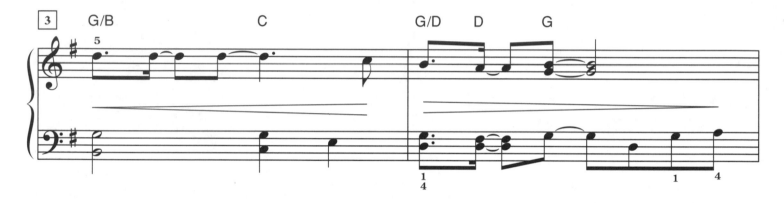

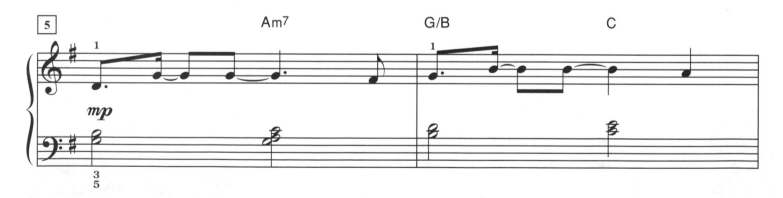

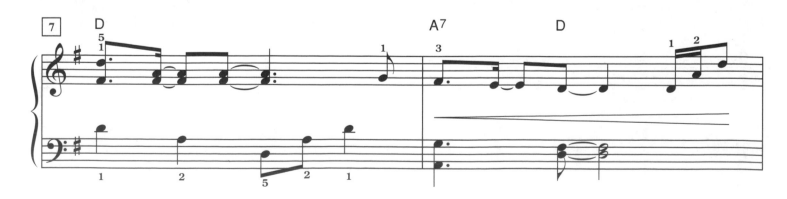

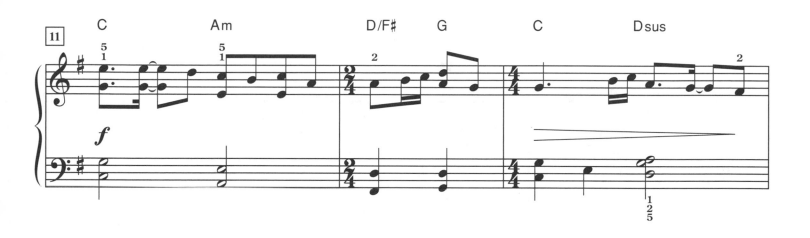

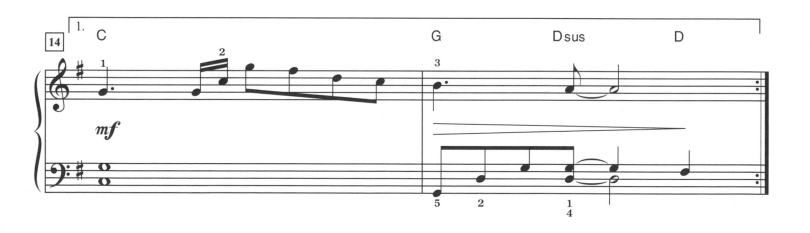

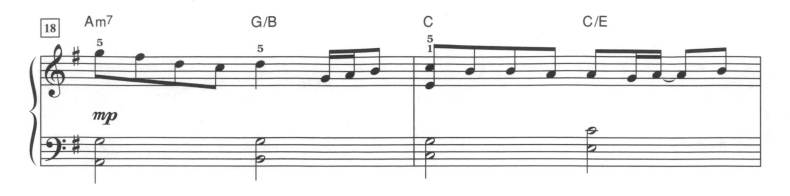

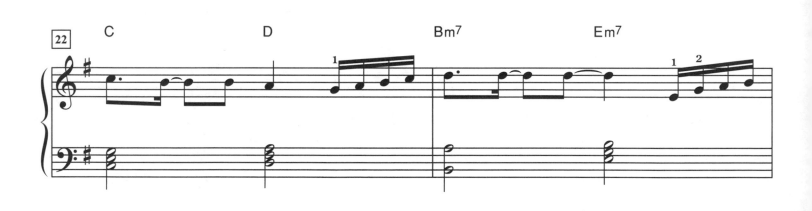

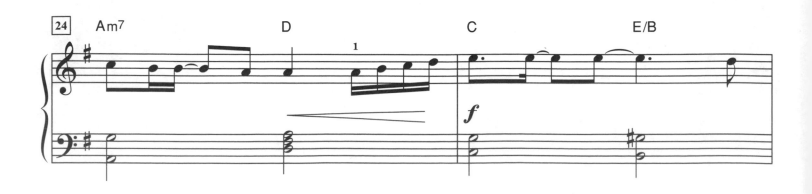

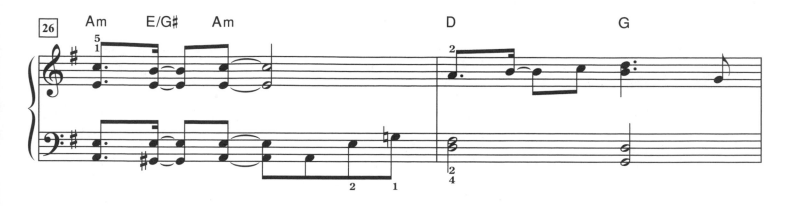

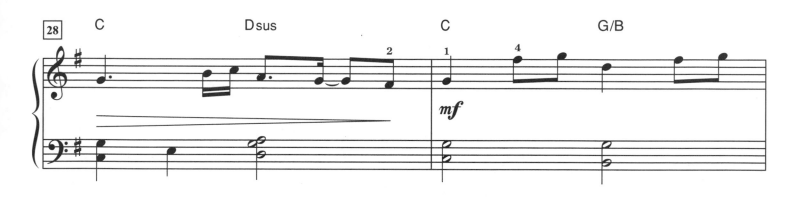

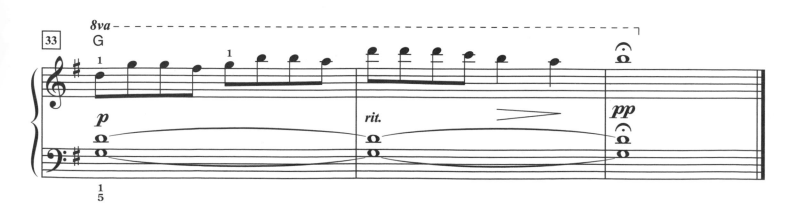

IF YOU BELIEVE

Written by Jim Brickman
Arranged by Dan Coates

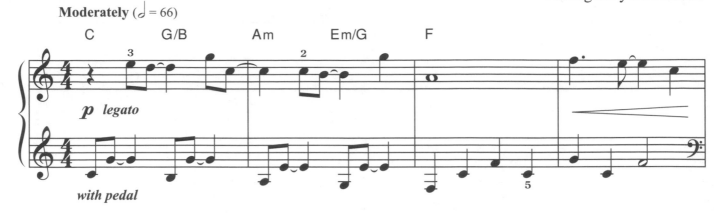

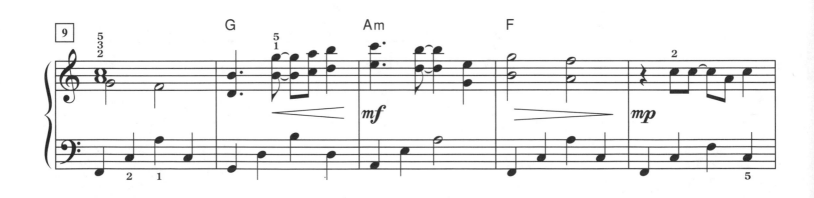

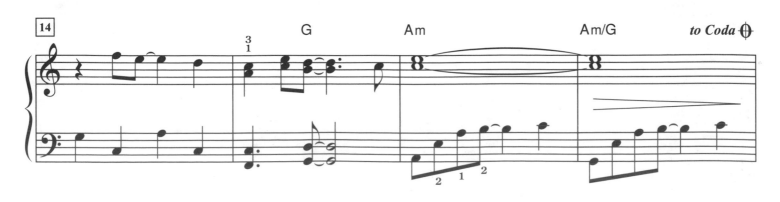

JOY TO THE WORLD

Traditional
Arranged by Jim Brickman
Arranged by Dan Coates

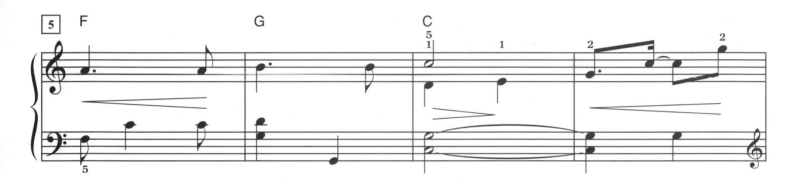

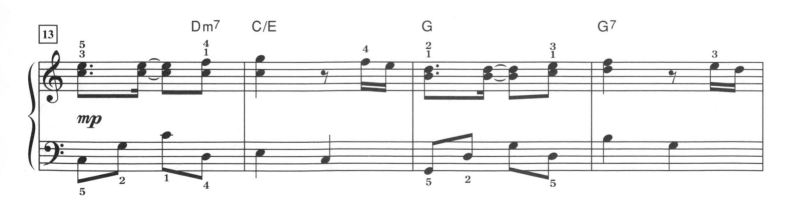

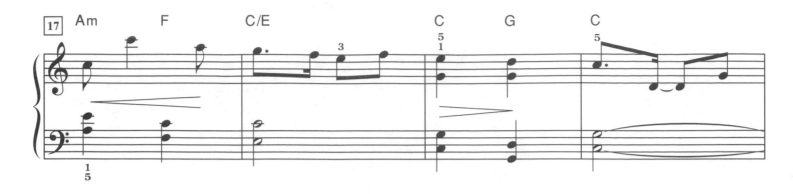

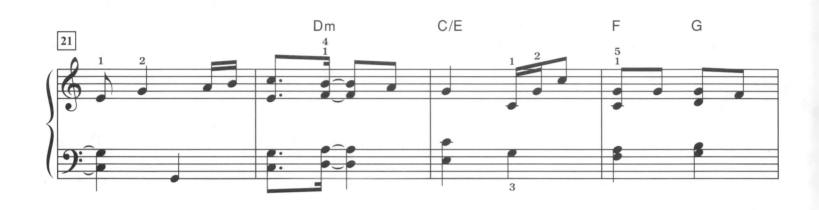

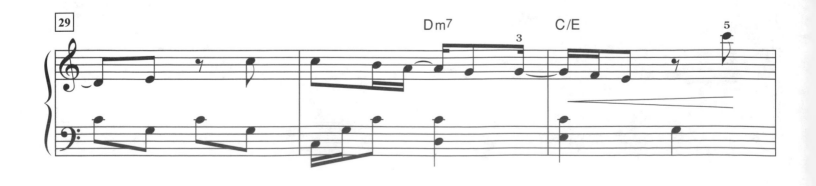

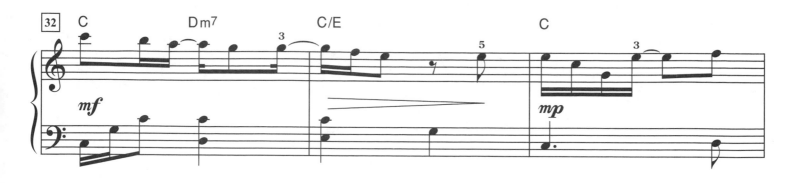

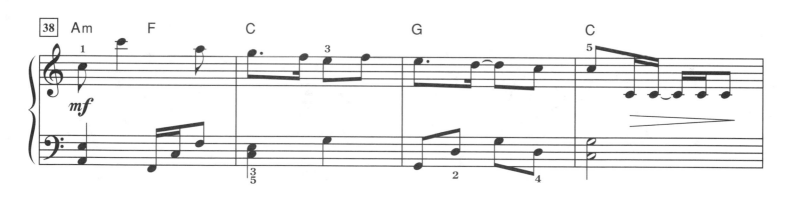

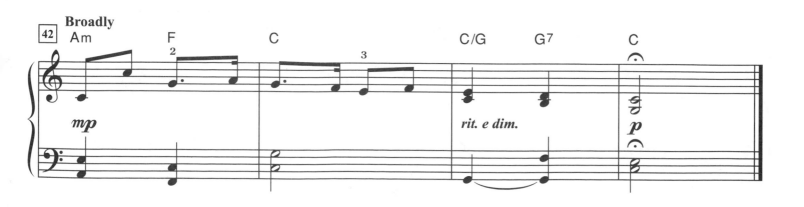

O HOLY NIGHT

By Adolphe Charles Adam
Arranged by Jim Brickman
Arranged by Dan Coates

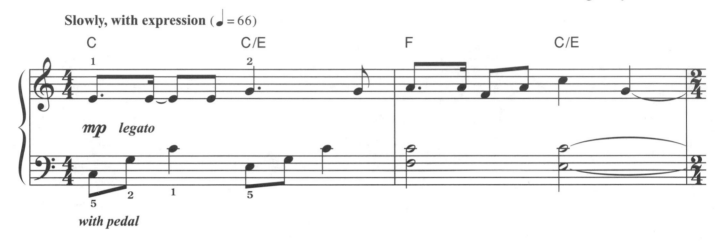

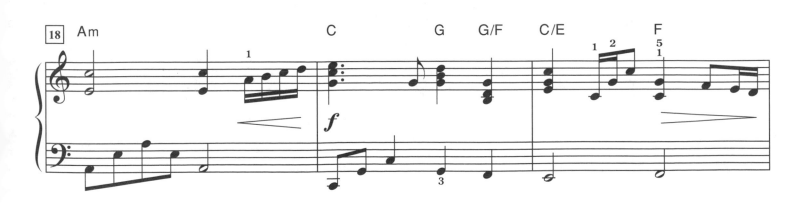

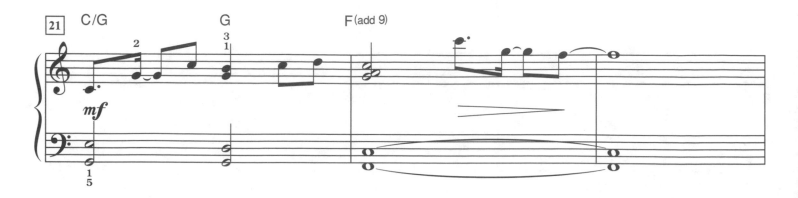

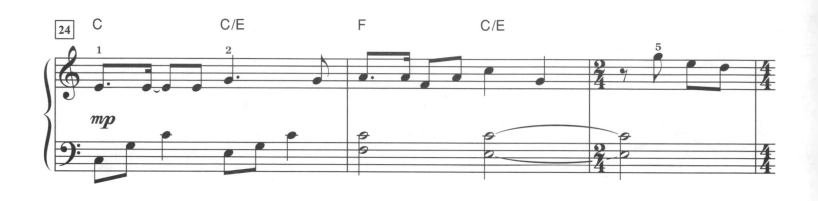

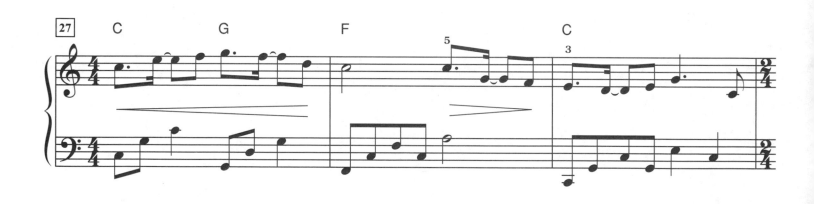

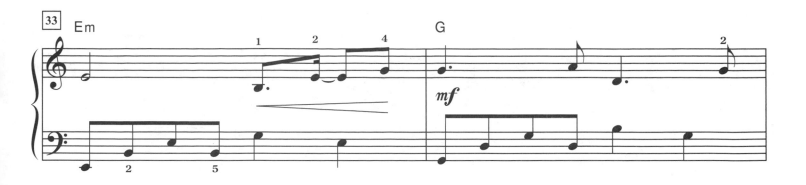

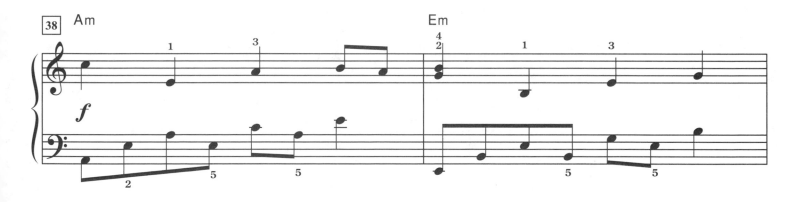

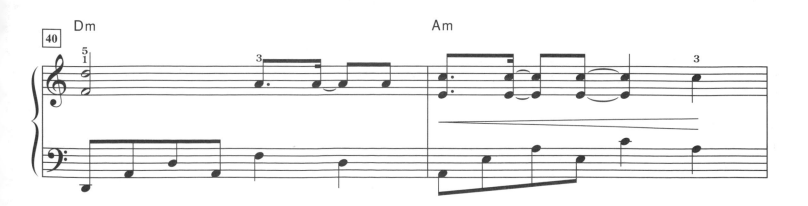

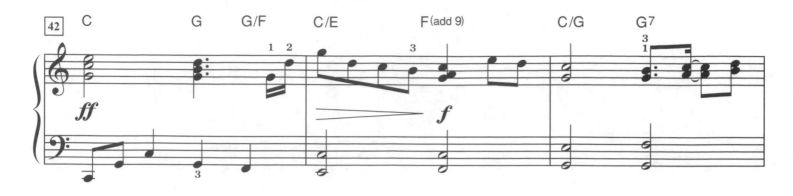

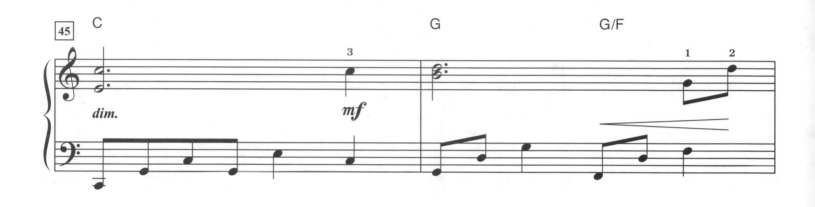

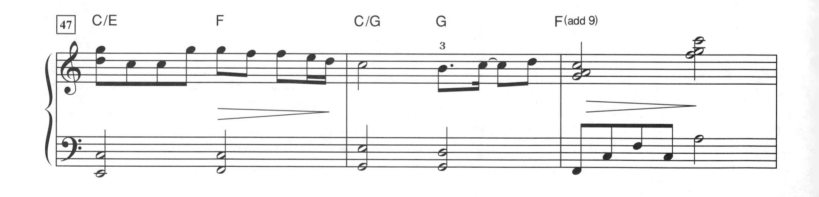

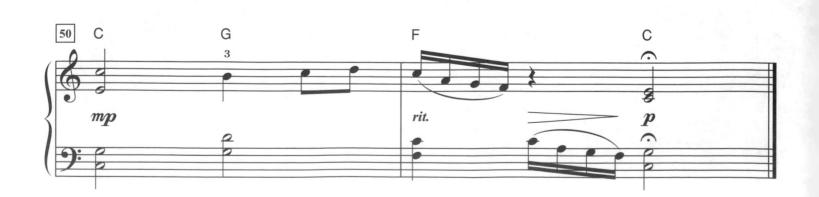

PEACE
(Where the Heart Is)

Words and Music by
Jim Brickman and Keith Follese
Arranged by Dan Coates

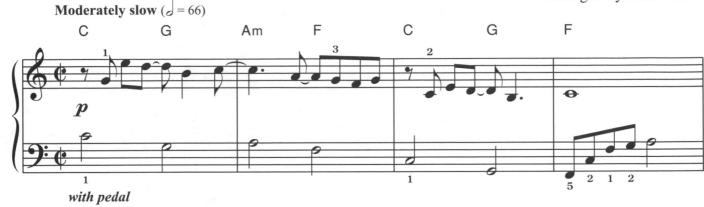

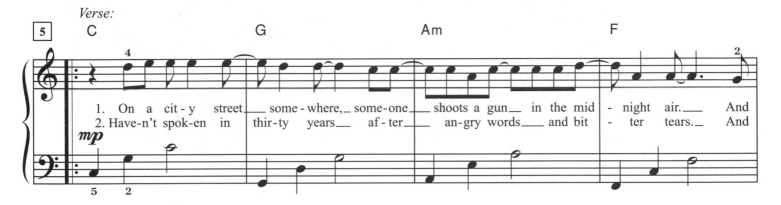

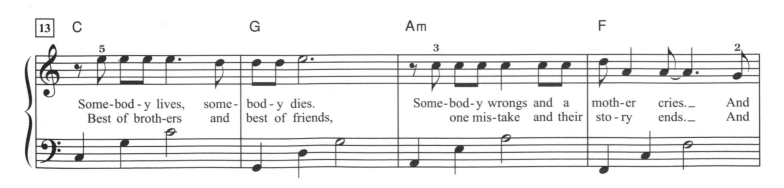

Hope is the some-thing that__ re-minds__ us, it's not too late__ to find__

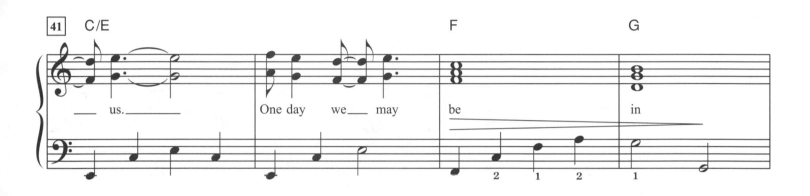

__ us.__ One day we__ may be in

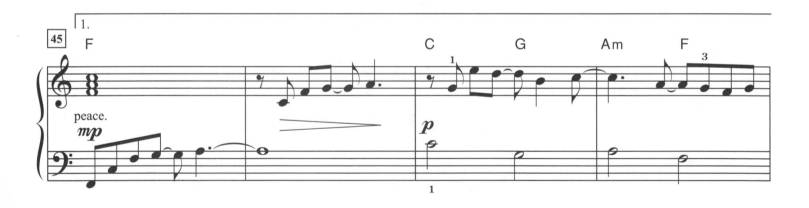

peace.
mp

peace. It's all a-bout__ for-give-
mp

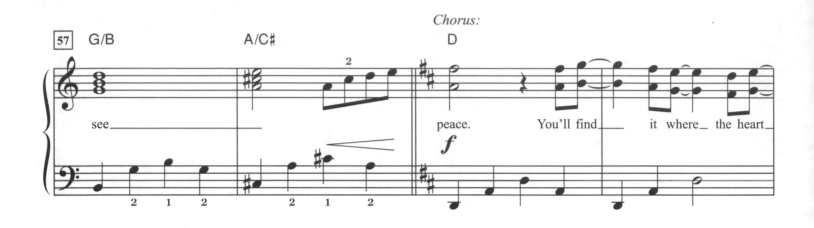

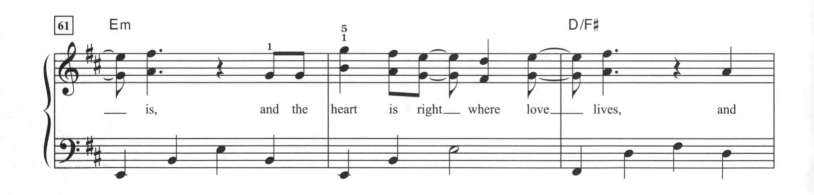

some-thing that_ re-minds_ us,   it's not too late_ to find_ us._

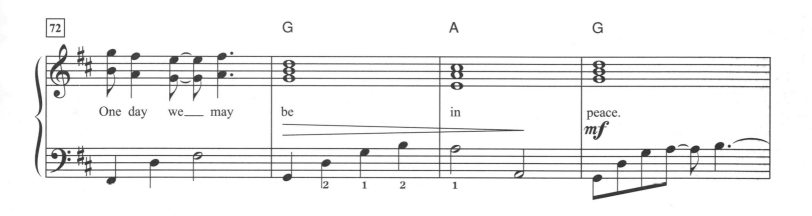

One day we_ may   be   in   peace.

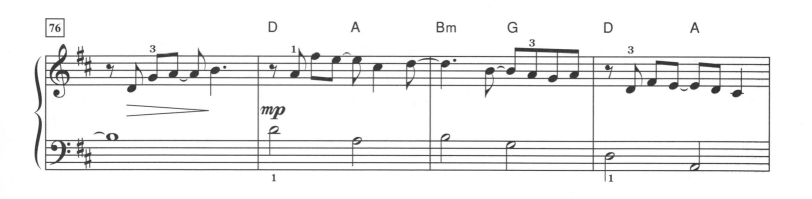

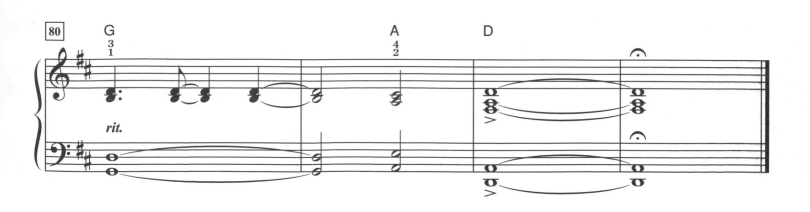

SENDING YOU A LITTLE CHRISTMAS

Words and Music by Jim Brickman,
Victoria Shaw, and Billy Mann
Arranged by Dan Coates

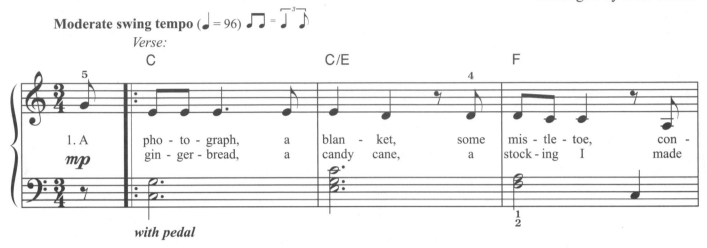

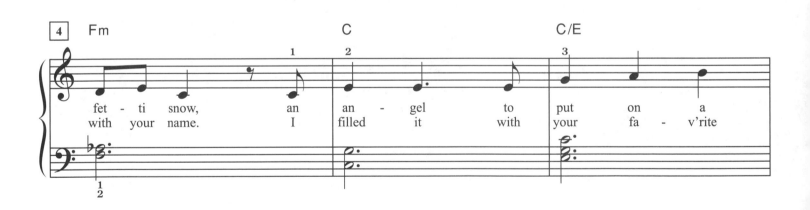

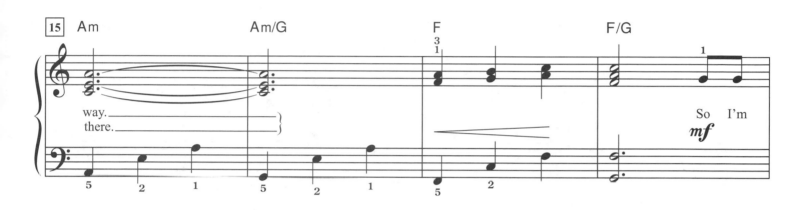

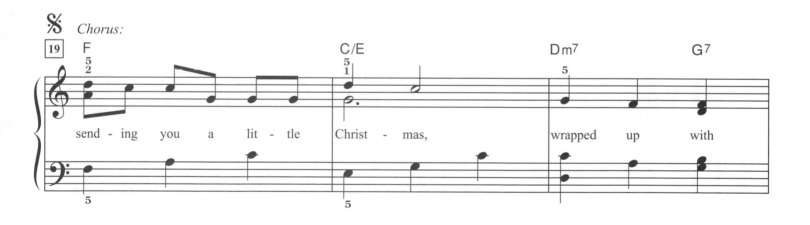

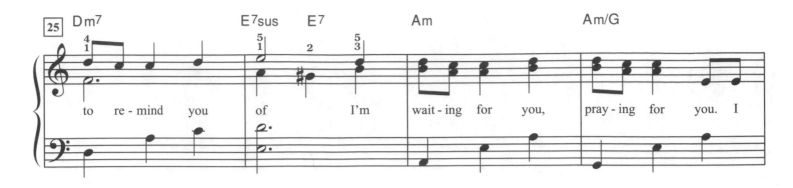

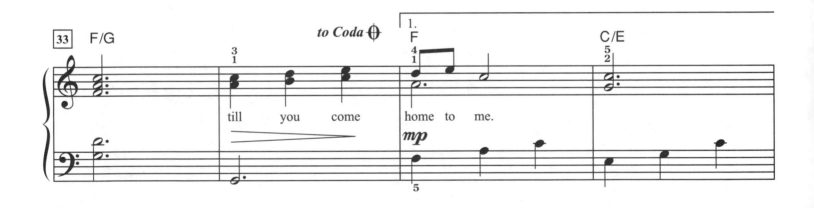

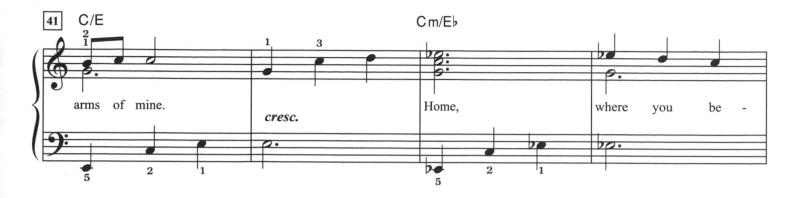

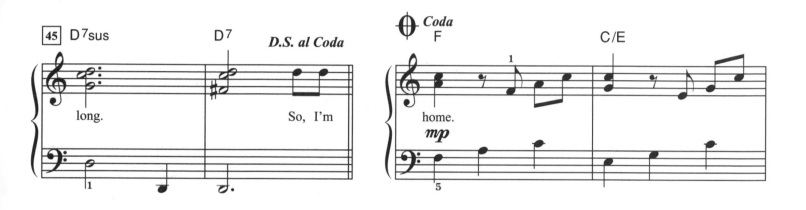

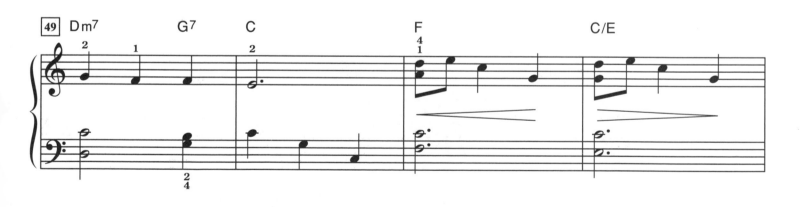

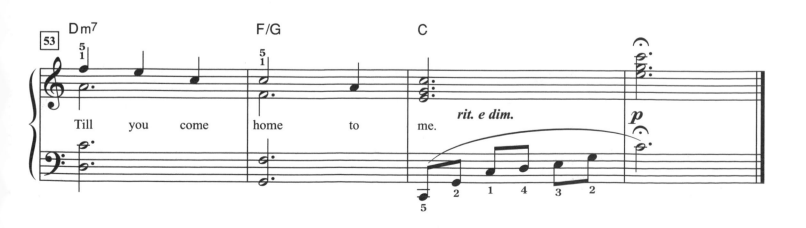

SILENT NIGHT

Words and Music by
Franz Gruber and Joseph Mohr
Arranged by Jim Brickman
Arranged by Dan Coates

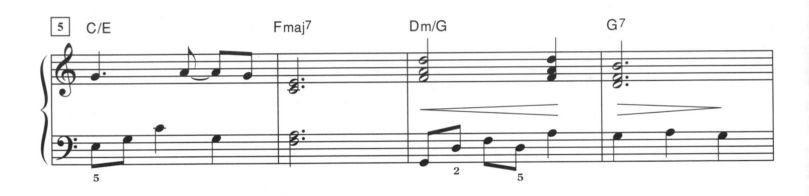

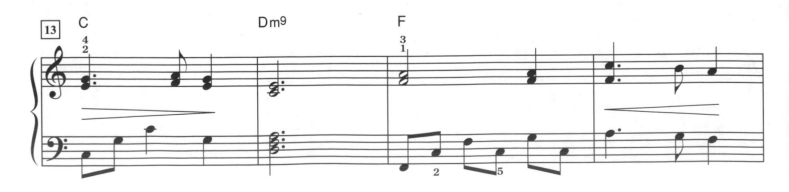

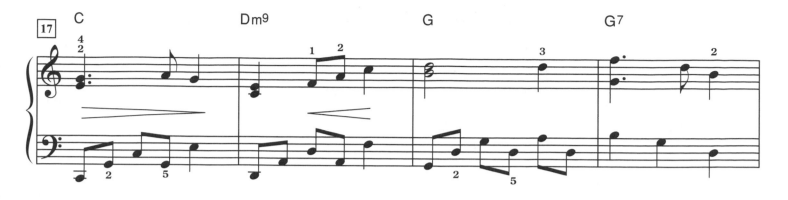

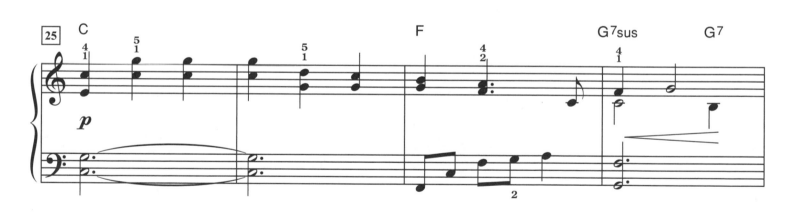

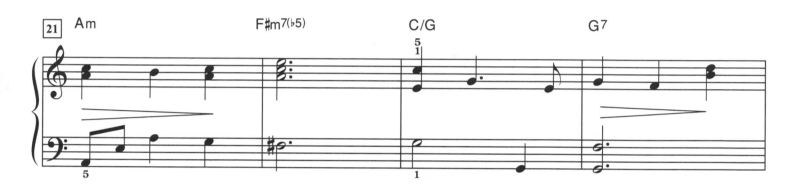

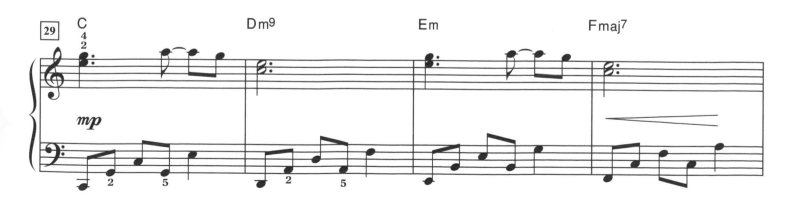

SNOWFLAKE

Written by Jim Brickman
Arranged by Dan Coates

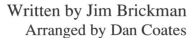

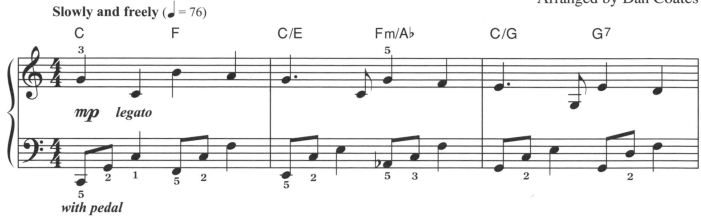

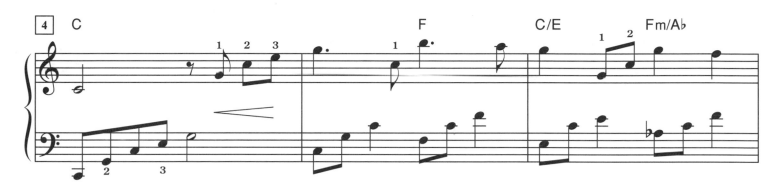

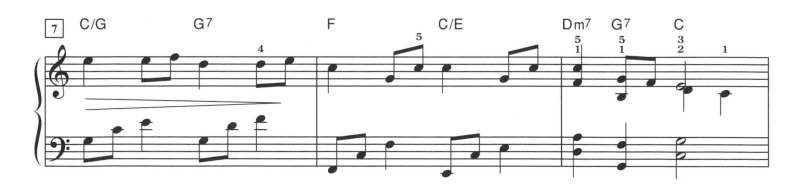

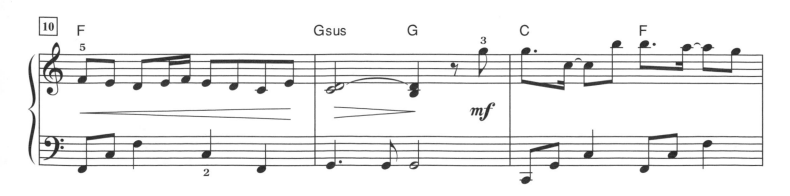

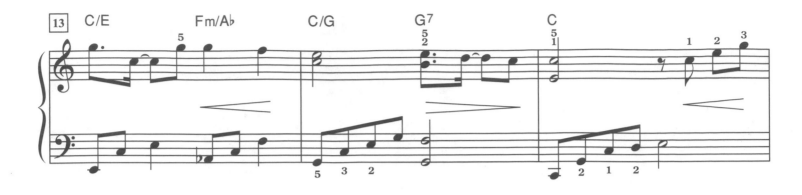

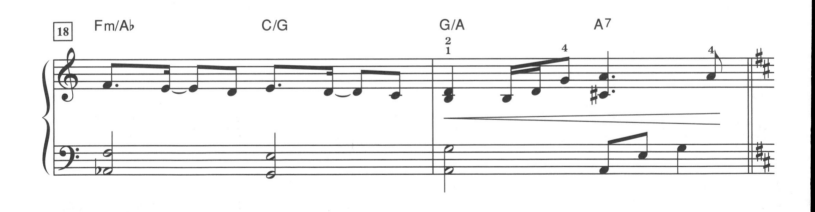

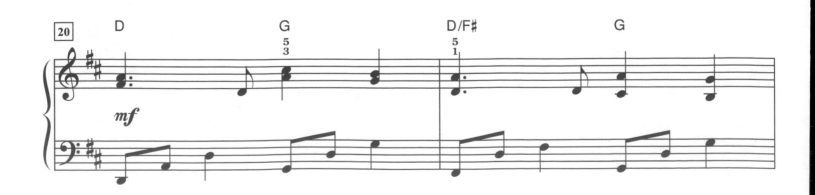

SILVER BELLS

Words by Ray Evans
Music by Jay Livingston
Arranged by Dan Coates

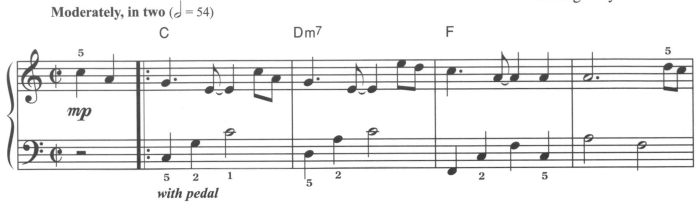

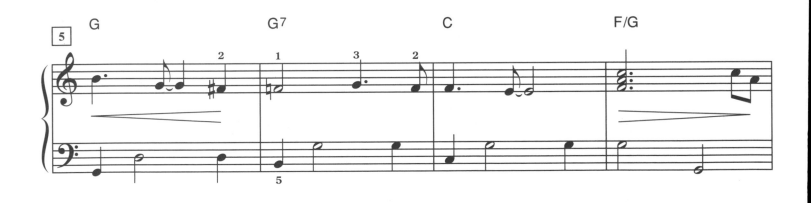

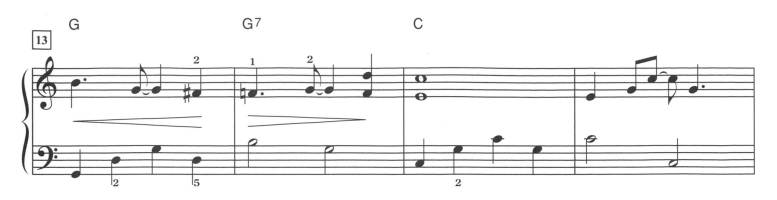

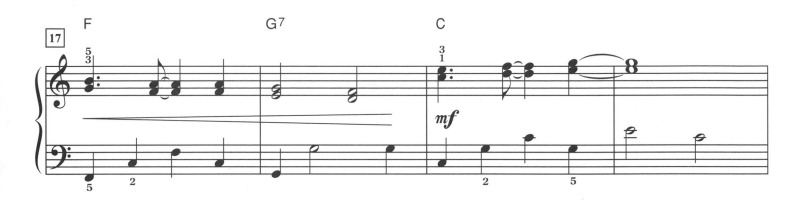

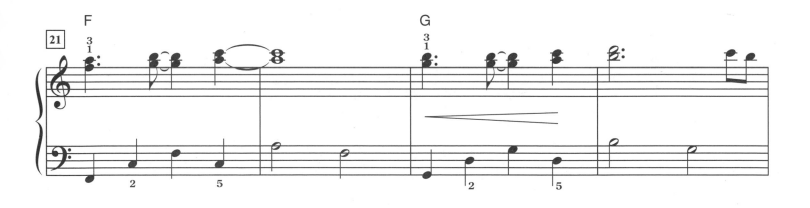

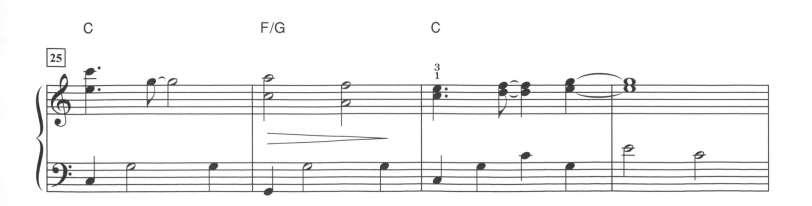

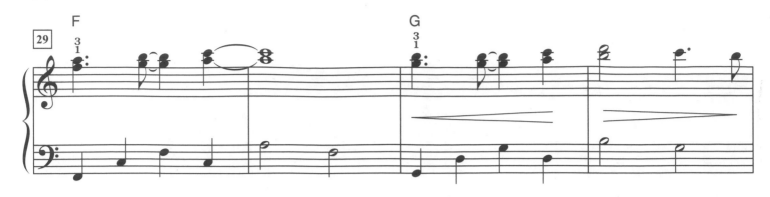

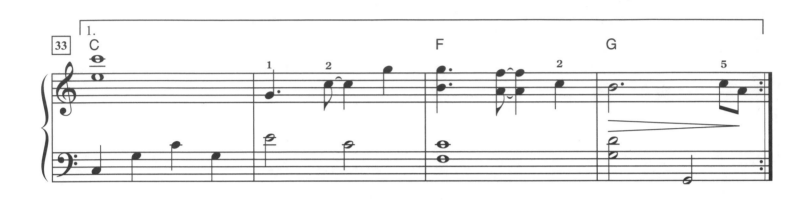

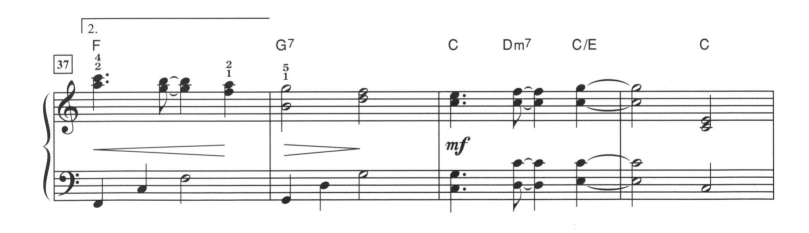

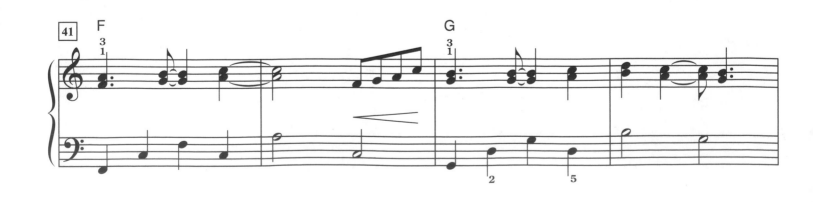

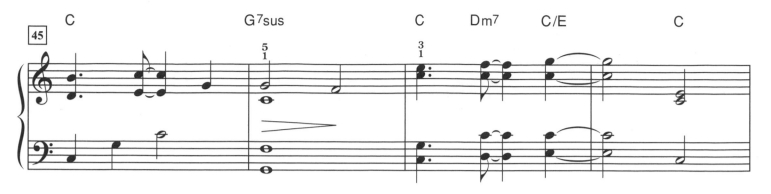

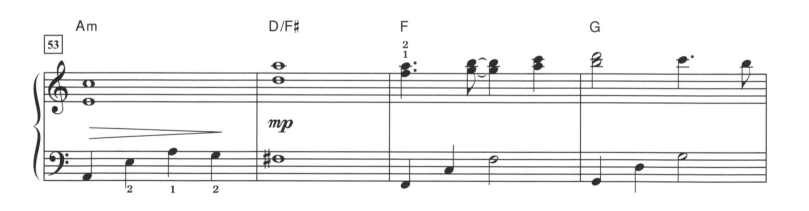

WINTER PEACE

Written by Jim Brickman
Arranged by Dan Coates

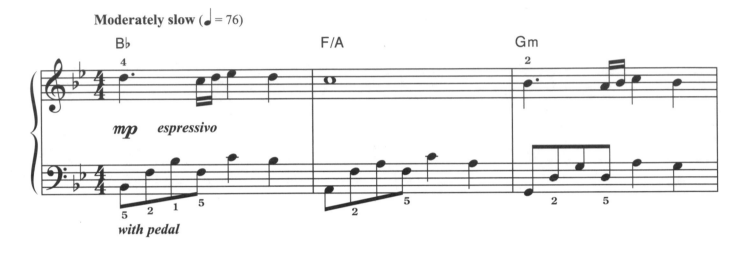

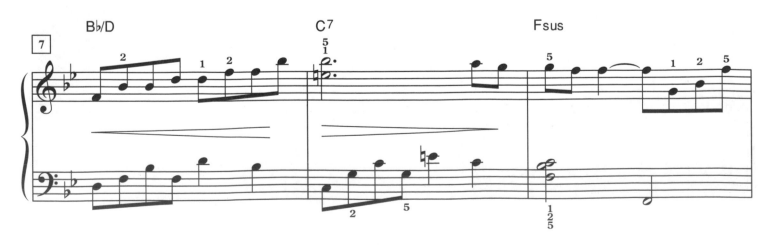

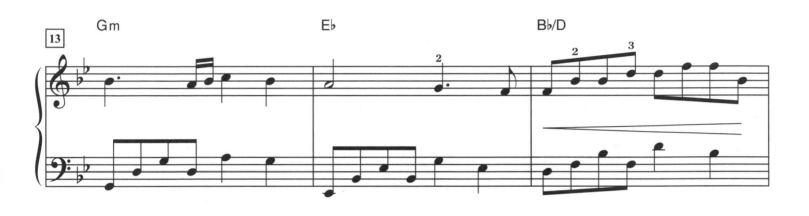

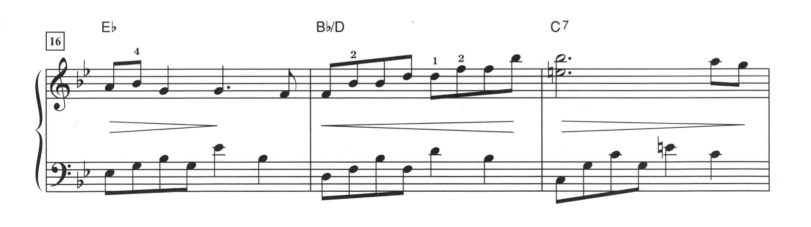

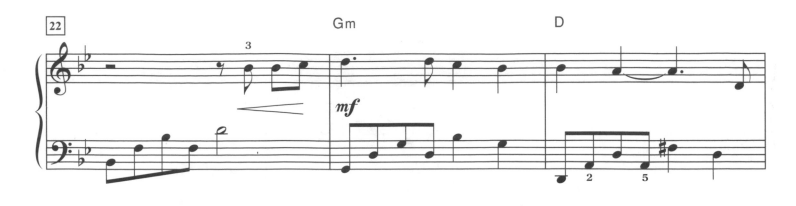

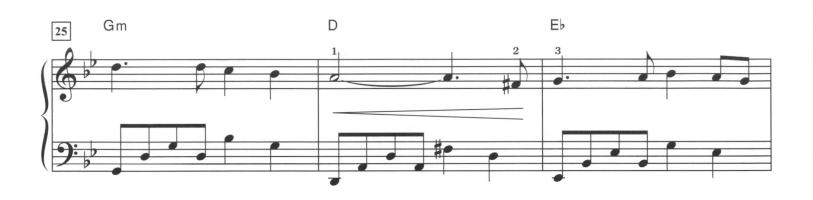

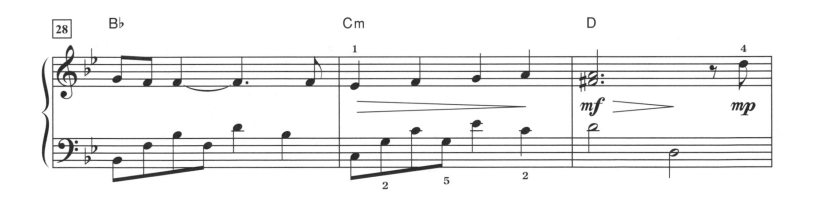

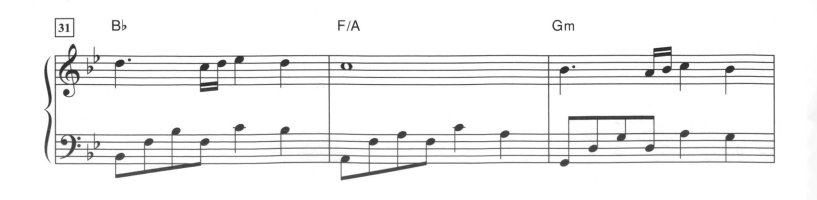

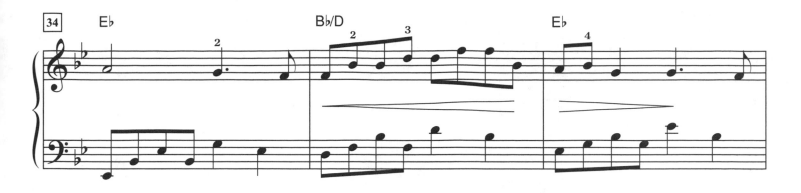

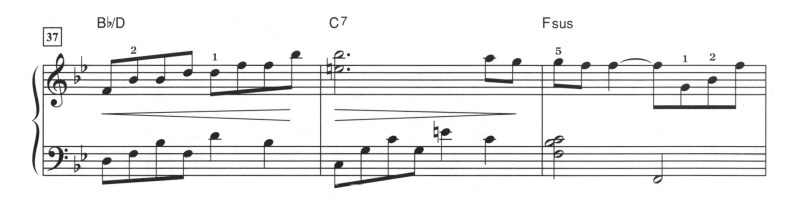

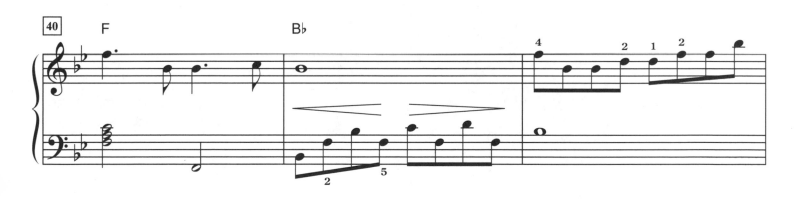

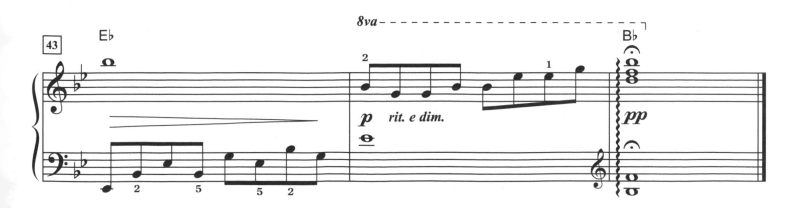

JOIN JIM'S VIP CLUB TODAY!

Being A VIP Member Includes The Following Benefits:

After Concert Meet-N-Greet Pass For Two

10% Discount On All Purchases from Jim's Online Store

VIP Brickman Tote Bag • VIP T-shirt, Keychain, Photo, Brickman Scrapbook

Brick Notes VIP Email-Newsletter • Online Interactive Message Board

Concert Ticket Pre-Sales • Exclusive VIP Merchandise

To Sign Up Today, Visit www.JimBrickman.com